Same Stories, Different Storytellers

Myth Patterns Across Civilizations

Natasha Cover

Same Stories, Different Storytellers

Warning and Disclaimer

Every effort has been made to make this book as accurate as possible. However, no warranty or fitness is implied. The information provided is on an "as-is" basis. The author and the publisher shall have no liability or responsibility to any person or entity with respect to any loss or damages that arise from the information in this book.

Publisher Contact

Skinny Bottle Publishing
books@skinnybottle.com

SKINNY BOTTLE

Note

Some of the religions discussed in this book are still active. Because this book focuses on early civilizations and their beliefs, all myths and stories are talked about in the past tense. No disrespect is intended to any religion, be it currently practiced or no longer believed in.

Author bio:

Natasha Cover is a student of history and mythology, having developed a love for both at an early age. In her spare time, she enjoys writing, geeking out about all things nerdy, and learning about the religions of ancient societies. Sometimes the three coincide. To learn more about her passion for mythology, or for updates on her books, visit her at

mythdancer.blogspot.com

Introduction

Since the beginnings of mankind, there have been stories. History, fantasy, interweaving of fact and fiction; stories containing these exist in the modern world just as much as they did in ancient times. Storytellers weave elaborate tales about that which they do not understand. Through their stories, they attempt to explain the inexplicable. Decades ago concepts such as mobile communication, the internet, and space travel seemed far-flung and impossible. Yet, as science advanced, explanations became available. What was once fiction was explained through facts. The same holds true of tales from early civilizations. Where once gods and monsters were the explanation for natural phenomena such as earthquakes or the plague, science has since offered more logical explanations.

Yet across cultures there exist tales with startling degrees of similarity, particularly when the societies who told them had little to no contact with one another. Some of these similarities are easily explained. For instance, civilizations which existed near volcanoes frequently had angry fire deities in their myths and legends. People who lived on islands often believed myths about the land being raised from the sea by early gods and goddesses. These common myths can be explained based on the circumstances and geography of the people who created them.

However, other similarities are more difficult to explain. Numerous civilizations with little to no contact or trade with one another each feature the same concepts in their myths. Fierce dogs stand as guardians at the entrance to the underworld. A trio of women wield immense power and hold the fate of the world in their hands. A catastrophic flood sweeps over the land, destroying everything except for one family, warned by the gods. The sun suffers some catastrophic calamity, causing harm to the earth. Tricksters wreak mischief upon mankind and gods alike.

How can these eerily homogeneous myths be explained? In some cases, a historical event of great significance may have led to the development of similar stories across cultures. In others, perhaps these similar stories point to something within the mind of mankind – something which leads to abstract concepts being rationalized and explained in the same way throughout many different civilizations. The inexplicable is simplified to be understood in terms of those who created the stories. Because of this, myths can offer a look into the beliefs and circumstances of early societies. They show what was important, what was feared, what was revered, and what was to be avoided. These ancient stories paint a picture of the peoples who believed them – and their similarities show just how alike all of mankind is.

Fire

One story found time and again across cultures is the discovery of fire. An integral part of life for early peoples, fire was given great importance in their myths. It was equally important to their development. The discovery of fire led to the advancement of ancient civilizations. This miraculous element provided light and warmth, and improved food and shelter. It could be the centerpiece of a home, or a torch to act as a beacon in the darkness. Many civilizations tell stories of the discovery of fire. It was something to be coveted and prized, and once discovered, its secret could never be lost. Perhaps because fire was so powerful and provided so many options to those who possessed it, many civilizations attribute it as a gift stolen from the gods.

In Greek mythology, it was the Titan Prometheus who stole fire and gifted it to mankind. The first men were created by Prometheus, molded out of clay and made to walk upright with their faces turned towards the heavens. Zeus was fearful of man and refused to give them knowledge of fire. He was afraid that with it they might one day rival the gods. Because they were denied the gift of fire, early man was little better than animals.

Unable to cook, they ate raw meat. With no warmth during the night, they were forced to sleep bundled in furs for warmth. Darkness kept them confined once the sun went down, and so they were forced to live their lives only during the day.

Yet Prometheus saw past mankind's primitive nature and had hope for their future. He believed that if they could be taught and nurtured, they could be peaceful equals to the gods. As such, the Titan decided to steal fire and gift it to mankind. He snuck into the heart of Olympus, home of the gods, and stole an ember from the fire. Prometheus managed to smuggle this tiny spark out of Olympus without any of the gods noticing. He gifted it to man and taught them how to kindle it and care for it. The Titan taught mankind how to use fire to cook, and to make burnt offerings to the gods. He showed them how to craft pots and metal with flame, and how its light and warmth made living easier. Under the tutelage of Prometheus mankind grew in knowledge and in wisdom – but also in power.

Zeus, seeing this, again feared for the sovereignty of the gods. He punished Prometheus for his theft by chaining him to a rock. Every day a giant eagle, the holy symbol of Zeus, swooped down and devoured Prometheus' liver. The Titan's immortality meant that his liver regenerated with each dawn. Unable to die of his wounds, he lived countless lifetimes in pure, unending agony before a hero freed him.

As for mankind, Zeus could not take away their knowledge of fire – but he could cripple them, preventing them from ever equaling the gods. To this end, he crafted the first woman, Pandora. He tasked the other deities with bestowing upon her gifts of great beauty and charm. Pandora was wed to Epimetheus, the brother of Prometheus, and given a box as part of her dowry. She was warned that she should never open it. Curiosity eventually got the better of the woman, and she took a peek within the box. Immediately poverty, sickness, jealousy, old age, and every manner of vice swept out of the casket, darkening the world and the souls of mankind forever. Only hope remained, trapped within the box when Pandora slammed the lid closed. In this way, Prometheus' gift of fire helped to advance mankind, but Zeus' curse of mortality and hardship held them back from attaining divinity to equal the gods.

A story akin to this exists in Polynesian mythology, which attributes the theft of fire to the demigod Maui. Numerous tales exist of the exploits of this folk hero, who was responsible for raising the very islands his people called home and taming the sun to give them light. This was not enough for Maui, who wanted to make humanity as comfortable as possible – or at least to satisfy his need for adventure, for he was also a trickster with an insatiable curiosity. One day this curiosity made Maui decide to figure out where fire came from. He decided to approach the fire goddess Mahuika.

Mahuika made her home inside a cavern within a great mountain. Though a solitary deity, she welcomed Maui into her domain, for he was a distant descendant of hers. Maui pleaded with her on the behalf of mankind. He spoke of their plight without warmth and light to live by, without heat with which to cook their meals. Maui begged the goddess to give him fire so that he could gift it to humanity. His words moved her. In response, Mahuika plucked one of her fingernails, an ember, and gave it to Maui. The demigod left with her gift.

Yet curiosity got the better of Maui. He wanted to know where Mahuika's fire came from, and what would happen if she had no more sparks of flame. The demigod extinguished her fingernail and went back to the fire goddess' cave. When he explained that a mishap had led to the flame going out, Mahuika gifted him another of her nails. This continued until only two nails were left.

By this point, Mahuika realized that she had been tricked. In a rage she threw one nail at Maui, sparking a massive firestorm. The demigod shapeshifted into a bird and tried to escape her wrath, but the flames surrounded him. He prayed to the gods for aid. A deluge of rain appeared in answer to his prayer, putting out the fires. As soon as the rain disappeared Mahuika threw her last nail at Maui in the hopes of revenge. Her throw missed, however, and instead, the nail landed among the trees surrounding her mountainous home. When Maui saw how the trees caught flame he at once knew the secret of fire. He took two branches from a dry tree and returned to mankind. There he showed the villagers how to rub the wood together to produce a spark, and how to kindle and grow the fire. The gift of the flames allowed them to cook and craft, offering them more possibilities than they had ever before possessed. In this way, the trickster Maui aided humanity through the gift of fire.

Various Native American tribes believed that it was Coyote who stole fire and gave it to mankind. In some myths, he is painted as a benevolent deity who took pity on mankind. In others, Coyote himself was cold, and so he set out to steal fire to warm himself. Coyote traveled to a distant mountain where three fire sisters lived around their fire. They guarded the flames day and night. When they first heard Coyote they were worried that he was a thief, but upon seeing the seemingly ordinary coyote they took no notice of him. Because of this, Coyote was able to observe the firewomen carefully.

The cunning god noticed that there was one point during the early morning when the firewomen were tired, and so they guarded the fire less carefully. He determined that this was the best time to strike. Coyote crept away from the campsite and gathered many woodland creatures around him. In some versions of the myth it was all the birds that he summoned to aid him; in others, it was a mix of birds, frogs, chipmunks, and squirrels. The animals took pity upon the humans and their lack of fire. They agreed to help Coyote steal the flames and give them to mankind.

Coyote returned to the campsite of the three firewomen. Again, they were nervous at the sound of his approach, thinking him a thief. Again, they saw only a wild animal, and so let their guard down. Before dawn two of the sisters changed watch. They were tired, and so moved slowly. Coyote, seeing his moment, struck. He dashed towards the fire and seized a branch in his mouth. He bounded away with great speed. The firewomen pursued him, shrieking with rage. They came close to Coyote, close enough to seize his tail. Where their flaming hands touched his fur went white – and this is why coyotes have white-tipped tails to this day. Coyote threw the branch to one of the other animals.

In one version of the myth, the fire was eventually passed between all the animals. The fire sisters caught up to them one at a time, each time raking their hands across the animal. This burning touch caused the squirrel's tail to curl, the chipmunk's back to gain stripes, and the frog's tail to fall off. At last the animals passed the fire to a tree. The firewomen surrounded the tree and begged and pleaded with it to return the flame but were unable to reclaim it. They turned to violence then, attacking the tree in an attempt to force it to give up the fire. Yet the tree stood strong and would not give up its prize. Defeated, the fire sisters returned to their camp. Yet Coyote with his trickery was smarter than they were, and knew how to coax fire out of the tree. The god took two dried branches from the tree and approached a human village. There Coyote showed the mortals how to rub the sticks together to produce fire. The flames were now stored in all dried wood and could be conjured whenever mankind needed.

In another version of the story, the burning branch was passed from bird to bird. Each eventually grew exhausted and was forced to pass the torch off to the next animal. In the end, it was the hummingbird who fluttered desperately with the fire. Yet as Coyote and the birds fled their pursuers, the flames began to die. Desperate to escape, Coyote took the branch back from the hummingbird and sought shelter in a large cave. The fire seemed to have died, and he worried that it had all been for naught. Desperate, Coyote blew and blew upon the stick he held. Eventually, a small spark caught, and the flames began to grow. He fed it kindling all through the night until his pursuers gave up and returned home. Then Coyote took the fire to a nearby village. He taught the humans there how to create a flame, and how to tend to it. Coyote's gift of fire was of great benefit to humanity.

Fire was an astoundingly potent tool for early mankind. Because of this, the idea of it being a gift from the gods makes sense. Yet what is it about fire which made multiple cultures consider it something to be stolen from the gods? It was frequently depicted as something to be pilfered, its thief pursued or punished by those who had owned the flames. Rarely did myths depict fire being given freely to mankind. Was this because fire was deemed too powerful to be gifted to those who did not already possess it? Or did mankind think as Zeus did: That any knowledge which might raise humanity to a level near divinity was too dangerous to be given into their hands?

Certain regions of Africa tell a story about the origins of fire, in which only select individuals were deemed responsible enough for the flames. In their hands, it was a tool, but in the hands of the untrained or foolish, fire could lead to calamity. The story tells of a hunter who saw a mysterious cloud on the horizon. He followed it until night fell, at which point he was surprised to find a warm glow in the same spot on the night sky/ After traveling for some time he reached the source of the light and smoke – a large fire. Having never seen anything like it before, the hunter bowed before the flames and offered them obeisance.

The fire was pleased by the hunter's manners. Because of his kindness, it offered to cook his meat for him and provide him with a warm place to stay the night. In exchange, the flames requested that he feed it some of the nearby wood and grass. The hunter readily agreed, and they spent a comfortable night together. In the morning the hunter offered the fire a trade. He would take it back to his village and use it for cooking, warmth, and light; in exchange, he would keep the fire well fed. But the fire refused this offer, insisting that it was too dangerous. If anything went wrong, it could destroy villages and forests alike. The fire made the man swear to secrecy before he left to return home.

The hunter kept his word and told no one about the fire's existence – not even his wife. However, he shared some of his cooked meat with her. Both found the taste far preferable to raw meat. His wife asked where he had come by such a thing, but he refused to tell her. Several times after that the hunter returned to the fire, each time coming home with more cooked meat. One day the wife could stand her curiosity no longer. She tasked a neighbor with following her husband. When the second man saw the fire and learned of its potential, he was overcome with rash greed. He seized a branch in his hand and ran back to the village. As he ran, the branch in his hand trailed fire all the way.

When the hunter awoke it was to a landscape on fire. His careless neighbor had started a conflagration which had consumed much of his surroundings. Many of the villagers died before they were able to reach a river. Those who managed to cross it were safe thanks to the boundary of the water but had to watch as their homes burned to ashes.

The hunter saw all of this with sorrow and listened as the fire counseled him. It warned that the secret of fire was now known to mankind. If used properly, and treated with respect, it could be a tool to aid humanity. If used in carelessness, the fires would consume and destroy everything that they touched. So, it was that fire itself offered a cautionary tale about its existence and its dangers.

When treated and tended to properly, fire was an integral part of the home, a benevolent entity which made life possible. Because of this, for many cultures fire embodied the hearth and the home. It was a central part of their home life, the part of the house around which everything else revolved. It bound together the family and made their everyday activities possible.

In Slavic mythology, three fire deities were worshipped. Each of these gods pertained to a different aspect of fire. Svarog, the god of the forge flame, had two sons: Dazbog, god of the flaming sun, and Svarozhich, god of the hearth flame. As Catholocism entered Russia and became the dominant religion, pagan practices revolving around the old gods were modified to fit with the new faith of the Russians. Old deities gradually lost their roles and importance. However, smaller, less powerful entities erupted in folktales and were believed in by many. Worship practices of Svarozhich and the hearth fire were converted into reverence for creatures known as domovoi.

The domovoi were described as tiny old men covered in black, sooty hair. They lived in the stoves and hearth fires of Russian homes. They were said to be quiet spirits who largely kept to themselves. However, a domovoi would always look out for his family and care for their health and wellbeing. Stories describe the domovoi as being grandfatherly and kind, and exceptionally loyal to their families. If the man of the house left for a journey, the stove door was closed to ensure that the domovoi would not follow him. When a family moved to a new house, an ember from the old stove was transplanted into the new hearth, ensuring that the domovoi would remain with the family.

If a family were foolish enough to offend a domovoi, the spirit could turn capricious and cause all manner of mayhem for its hosts. Meals would burn, bread would not cook, or the horses – an animal the domovoi was said to be especially fond of – would go mad in their stables and escape. In other cases, the domovoi would simply leave the unworthy family, taking his blessings somewhere where he would be better appreciated. The family who offended the domovoi was foolish indeed. They lost all their luck, and a faithful spirit who would have stayed with their family for generations. Because of its long-term loyalty, possession of a domovoi was something to be cherished and proud of. They brought good health and luck to their families for so long as they remained with them.

For the ancient Greeks, it was Hestia who embodied the spirit of hearth and home. One of the oldest deities in Greek mythology, Hestia was the sister of Zeus, Poseidon, Hades, Demeter, and Hera. Her brothers ruled over mighty forces such as the air, the sea, and the underworld; her sisters had domain over the harvest, and marriage and childbirth. The fact that the Greek myths painted Hestia as their sibling implied that the home and family were every bit as important as those other, mighty forces. Even more telling was the fact that Hestia was the firstborn of her siblings – born before even Zeus, chief among the gods. Few myths exist about Hestia, yet she was depicted in numerous paintings and carvings. She sat among the other gods on Mount Olympus. At that heavenly flame, she made offerings and ensured that the hearth fire of the gods was kept lit and well-tended. The first offering of every meal in the home was given to Hestia in honor of her importance.

The Roman version of Hestia, Vesta, was given even more importance than her Greek counterpart. A massive fire was kept forever burning in the temple of Vesta. This fire was tended to by her virgin priestesses all year round. The fire represented Rome, the ultimate home to which all Romans owed their duty and allegiance. So long as the flames remained burning, Rome was blessed and would be prosperous. Should they ever be extinguished, calamity would follow. It was believed that if the fires of Vesta went out, the gods' favor had turned from Rome, and as such was taken as a serious portent of disaster. Yet so long as the fire burned, Vesta watched over and blessed Rome. All paid homage to her, no matter how mighty the hero – including Romulus and Aeneas, two of the greatest legends of Rome.

Vesta was also inextricably tied to the origins of the Roman Empire. One of her priestesses, a Vestal Virgin by the name of Rhea Silvia, was impregnated by the Mars, the god of war. Her children were Romulus and Remus. The boys grew up to overthrow a tyrant and reclaim their birthright as rulers. Though Remus was killed in a quarrel with Romulus over who should rule, his brother would go on to found Rome itself. In this myth, Vesta's importance to the city was established even before Rome existed.

The Hindu god Agni oversaw hearth and home in a manner similar to Hestia and Vesta. In addition to being a god of the hearth flame, Agni also represented the sacrificial flames, the fires of death and rebirth, and both lightning and the sun. Yet it was the hearth fire, and the light which he provided, which were the most revered aspects of Agni. An ancient Hindu festival called Diwali involved thousands of candles being lit to celebrate the triumph of light over darkness. Many of the ceremonies for this celebration involved Agni, for it was his light which resided in the candles and cast back the shadows of night.

In addition to all his other roles, Agni played a central part in Hindu wedding rituals. A fire was lit in the center of a circle, which the bride and groom walked around seven times while reciting their vows. Agni's flame stood as witness to their commitment to one another. His fire consecrated the marriage, binding the duo together with the purity of flame.

Hinduism revered Agni's fire as gentle and necessary for life – but myths from other parts of the world demonstrated that fire could also be dangerous. Such myths were particularly prominent in cultures who lived in proximity to active volcanoes. Numerous other mythologies describe violent fire gods whose wrath could lead to the destruction of entire cities. The deities these people described were a far cry from the gentle and peaceful hearth gods. Instead, they were often tempestuous, their temperaments ranging from still and quiet to explosive and furious.

Vesta was not the only fire deity in Roman mythology. Vulcan was revered as the god of the forge fire, as well as of volcanoes. Prayers and offerings were given to Vulcan in the hopes that he might stay his wrath. It was believed that his anger led to volcanic eruptions. It was during the reign of the Roman Empire that Mount Vesuvius erupted, resulting in the extinguishment of all life within Pompeii. Volcanoes were not uncommon within the reaches of Rome's rule. In Roman mythology, Vulcan was said to be a god with a fiery temper. Appeasing him could keep the people of Rome safe, but angering him was a calamitous idea.

Among the deities of Japanese mythology, known as the kami, there existed many fire gods. Some represented the tamer aspects of fire used in the home, such as for cooking. Yet among the most dangerous fire deity was Kagutsuchi, the fire god whose dismembered body became the very volcanoes of Japan. Kagutsuchi was the son of two of the first kami, Izanagi and Izanami. Izanami's pregnancy with him was filled with unbearable pain. When her labors began, Izanagi was horrified to see a child on fire emerging from his wife's womb. The searing agony of her delivery killed Izanami. Filled with grief and rage, Izanagi beheaded Kagutsuchi and chopped his son's body into pieces.

Each of those pieces fell into the sea. These fragments of Kagutsuchi's body became the volcanoes which form Japan's landmass.

Kagutsuchi's entrance into the world marked the beginning of death, for no one had died before Izanami. Because of this, Izanami would become the goddess of Yomi, the Japanese underworld. Fire is shown in this story to be powerful enough to destroy even the gods. Yet Kagutsuchi is not portrayed as capricious or malicious; it was not his intent to do his mother harm. Instead, the fires which consumed Izanami in childbirth were simply the nature of Kagutsuchi. One cannot expect fire to be anything other than what it is – a tool, but also dangerous to all.

Fire plays many roles in mythologies, just as it has multiple uses in real life. For each story told, there is an echoing story found in another culture. It is revered and necessary; it is dangerous and vicious. Ancient societies were fascinated with fire, perhaps because of its importance in their day to day lives. An examination of their mythologies and stories demonstrates how fire was viewed around the world.

Land

Most mythologies have a story about the creation and formation of the world. The most important part, aside from the creation of mankind, was the forming of the land. It is on land where life takes place, and so its creation is one of the integral parts of myths. Yet the land was rarely created first. In fact, for many cultures, land was the final element to be created. In several myths, the heavens and the seas already existed before the earth was formed.

In the Judeo-Christian book of Genesis, the creation took place solely through the words of God. He spoke and matter obeyed. First, the world and the waters were made; next came light, leading to day and night. The sky was formed to separate the world from what lay beyond. At last, God formed earth, separating the seas with landmasses. On these, He placed all manner of plants and vegetation.

The stories of the Yoruba tribe of Africa also place the creation of land after sea and sky. Olorun, chief of the gods, ruled over the sky; Olokun was the goddess of the sea. The gods lived in harmony in the heavens or in the murky marshlands below. Yet Obatala was not satisfied with this way of life. He dreamed of dry land, and of animals and people who inhabited it. Obatala went to Olorun and asked for permission to create earth. With Olorun's blessing obtained, Obatala began his efforts. He approached each god and asked for gold to make a chain. The gods willingly donated all the gold within heaven. With the help of a heavenly blacksmith, a mighty set of links was crafted from this gold, with a hook on one end. This hook was tethered to the edge of the sky. The chain was lowered slowly towards the ocean, and Obatala climbed down it.

But despite the generosity of the gods, there had not been enough gold in the heavens, and the chain did not reach all the way to the sea. Obatala hung at the end of the chain for a moment. He knew that the distance was too far to drop. He was saved by the advice of a prophet among the deities, who had told him what supplies to bring. Obatala raised a snail's shell he had filled with sand. He slowly poured the sand into the ocean below him. There it swirled in the sea and began to form a land mass. When the snail shell was empty, Obatala dropped a hen onto the pile of sand. The bird immediately began to scratch and peck, searching for food. As it did so, the sand was scattered by its feet. Everywhere the grains landed, new earth was created – hills and mountains, valleys and plateaus.

Obatala dropped off the chain and landed on the newly formed earth. He planted a palm nut in the soil. Immediately it sprouted and grew, and other trees quickly followed. Obatala made his home upon the land. Later humans and animals would be created and added to it. It was in this way that the Yoruba believed that the earth had been created.

The Japanese story of the creation of land is remarkably similar. In it, some of the islands of Japan are made by the gods, while others are born of them. Several generations of kami had already been born before two of the gods, Izanagi and his wife Izanami, stood on a bridge between heaven and the sea below. Using an ancient and divine spear the duo stirred the murky waters of the ocean. When they lifted the spear, the drops of brine which fell from its tip and landed in the water solidified into land. This became the first island of Japan.

Izanagi and Izanami descended from the bridge and settled upon the island, making it their home. They consummated their marriage. Despite some trials and tribulations, many children were born to the husband and wife. First came the four main islands of Japan; later, the smaller, outlying islands were birthed. Many of the divine spirits, known as the kami, which Japanese stories say inhabit trees, mountains, oceans, wind, and other natural phenomena, were also children of Izanagi and Izanami. The sun and the moon deities were also born of their union. Izanagi and Izanami's last-born child was Kagutsuchi. His birth was so violent that it tore Izanami apart from the inside, killing her with his fire. When Izanagi killed Kagutsuchi and dismembered him, his body parts became the volcanoes of Japan. The birth of Japan's volcanoes may have been violent, but the rest of the land's creation was a calm and natural process.

While the formation of land in many mythologies is peaceful, to the Polynesians it was a colossal struggle. Only their mightiest hero, the demigod Maui, was capable of raising up the islands upon which they made their homes. He did this with nothing but his strength. The story goes that one day two of Maui's brothers decided to go on a fishing trip. The demigod asked to accompany them and was welcomed onto their boat. It was a slow day, and no fish were biting. Bored and drowsy, both brothers began to doze off. Before they fell asleep, Maui asked them to remain very quiet. Any noises they made might scare off his catch. His brothers agreed but doubted that he would hook anything.

Yet Maui's fishing hook was no ordinary hook. Instead, it was the jaw of his dead grandmother, which he had retrieved and upon which he had performed many rituals and enchantments. Maui used some of his blood as bait and cast his hook into the ocean. Before long he had a catch – and it was something massive. He began to heave and tug, trying with all his might to pull up the taut string. The boat rocked and shook with his effort, waking up his brothers. Seeing that Maui had made a mighty catch, they began to row backward as fast as they could to help him. Bit by bit Maui dragged his catch upwards.

Then his brothers saw exactly what it was he had caught. It was no fish, but instead a giant land mass! Despite their oath of silence, the brothers exclaimed in shock. At once Maui's hook detached from the land, with it only partially pulled out of the water. Several Hawaiian stories say that the land fell off his hook a piece at a time, explaining the trail of islands. Many variations exist for the story, including what sort of hook was used, what made the brothers disturb Maui's efforts, and how the land came to be islands instead of a large land mass. Regardless of the specifics, most Polynesian tribes told the story of Maui fishing up the islands upon which they lived.

For some cultures, the creation of land was something easily accomplished. For others, it required ingenuity and effort.

In some cases, it was a struggle. Yet in most mythologies, it was the gods who formed the land after the heavens and the sea had already come into existence. What made early civilizations decide that this was the order in which the earth came into existence? To have humanity created after the earth makes sense, as mankind would need a place to live. But why have the seas and the skies made first?

Many ancient cultures viewed the sea as a ring which surrounded everything, ending at the edge of the sky. The ocean and the heavens were both unfathomable, their edges unable to be reached by early mankind. Land was more easily explored and understood. Perhaps this is part of why so many cultures believed it to have been crafted by the gods last. In addition, stories frequently tell of animals and mankind being created immediately after land. Sometimes the earth was formed solely to be populated. In other cases, the gods deemed the land too barren after its formation and decided to add humanity to it.

Whatever the reason, it is clear that many early societies viewed the earth upon which they dwelled in similar ways.

Dogs

Every society and culture has some belief of what happens after death. For some they believed in an afterlife; in others, a cycle of rebirth; still others believed that there was no life after death, only an ending, or a void of sorts. Yet for those societies who believed in an underworld or an otherworld of some kind, there often existed a creature tasked with guarding its entrance. Numerous mythologies from around the globe tell of a fearsome hound standing guard at the gate of the land beyond the living.

For the ancient Egyptians, this hound was known as Anubis. Egyptian mythology featured a pantheon of anthropomorphic animals, with the bodies of men and women, but the heads of fierce creatures. Anubis, the guardian of the afterlife, was depicted as possessing the head of a black jackal. Jackals are scavenger animals, and so it seems fitting that a jackal deity was associated with the dead. Anubis was not the god of the underworld in Egyptian mythology. Instead, that title belonged to Osiris, god of the dead. Anubis was a servant of Osiris, guarding the land that the king ruled over and overseeing the admission of new souls. In many tales, Osiris was Anubis' father, and the jackal deity's mother was Nepthys, a goddess who presided over funerary rites.

New souls entered the afterlife only after a test scrutinized by Anubis. The heart of the deceased was placed upon the scales of truth, counter measured by a feather. Should the heart of the dead weigh no more than the feather, a symbol of purity, their soul would be made immortal and would have blessings in the afterlife. However, if their heart was weightier than the feather, they were judged harshly. The heart would be tossed to a terrifying creature named Ammit. She was a fearsome goddess whose body was composed of parts of lion, hippopotamus, and crocodile. Ammit would devour the heart, condemning the soul to an existence without hope of the afterlife's immortality. Anubis could not be fooled or cheated, and would not show mercy, thereby allowing the scales to determine the fate of a person's soul.

Anubis was also viewed as a protector of the dead. One myth featured him standing guard over the body of Osiris while Osiris' wife Isis and Nepthys performed rituals to return him to life. Due to Anubis' role as a guardian of the deceased, statues and paintings of him were frequently included in grave sites, tombs, and pyramids. His name was also invoked in embalming and mummification rituals because of his role in Osiris' resurrection. Anubis was no ordinary hound, but an immensely powerful and intelligent deity.

In Norse mythology, there were several locations in the afterlife. The brave, including warriors and champions, were raised up to live among the gods. Some went to Odin's hall of Valhalla, while others dwelt in Freya's palace. This afterlife was full of feasting, drinking, and merriment. For cowards, thieves, and other wretched scum, death brought a more fearsome fate. They were condemned to the icy and nightmarish realm of Hel. This domain shared its name with the goddess in charge of it. Hel was the daughter of Loki and had been banished to the frigid wastelands as punishment by Odin. Her realm was a dreary, miserable place at best. At worst, it included eternal torture in the form of swords, snakes, poison, and drowning.

Standing guard over the realm of Hel was the hound Garmr. Said to be a pale hound with a blood-soaked chest and neck, Garmr kept watch over the kingdom of the dead. Only those who were dead could enter unless given permission by his mistress. Garmr also kept the souls of the dead from leaving the underworld. His howl struck terror into the hearts of all who heard it. There are two stories in which the gods entered Hel and crossed paths with Garmr. In one, Odin went to visit a dead seer. Though Garmr howled and growled at him, the mighty god was unafraid and continued his journey. In the other, Hermod, the messenger of the gods, entered the underworld to beg Hel to return a dead deity to life. Again, he was able to pass Garmr without hindrance. According to some stories Garmr's wrath could be soothed with an offering of a honey cake, or some other kind of sweet pastry. This idea of an appeasing gift being offered to a hound also appears in Greek and Roman mythology.

The most common story thread in Norse mythology is Ragnarok, the doom of the gods. Ragnarok prophesizes the coming of the end, in which the forces of Hel and the armies of the damned will rise, along with a massive army of fire giants, and destroy most of the gods. Very few will survive this apocalyptic event. In most of the stories the giant wolf Fenrir, another child of Loki, is fated to break free of his chains and kill Tyr, a god whose hand he had devoured when he was first entrapped by the gods. However, some versions of the myth attribute Tyr's death to Garmr, who will escape Hel and seek his vengeance upon the gods. There has been speculation that Garmr is simply another name for Fenrir, or that the two have been mixed up within the myths.

Perhaps the most well-known hellhound is Cerberus, the three-headed dog of Greek mythology. While his multiple heads are the most depicted feature of Cerberus, some accounts also give him the tail of a snake or have snakes emerging from all over his body. The Greek underworld is sometimes referred to as Hades, named for the god who rules over it. To enter Hades a dead soul had to cross the river Styx. To make this journey, coins needed to be offered as payment to Charon, the ferryman. Because of this, the dead were often buried with coins over their eyes. Once they had crossed the river Styx the dead soul would encounter Cerberus, who guarded the main entrance to the underworld. Much like Garmr, Cerberus' job was to keep the living out, and the dead inside.

Several myths involve Cerberus being overpowered or tricked into abandoning his guard post. The last of the twelve labors of Hercules was to capture Cerberus and bring him into the mortal world. With the help of Athena, goddess of wisdom, and Hermes, the god who escorted dead souls to Hades, Hercules was able to enter the underworld. He approached Hades and asked his permission to take Cerberus to the land of the living. Hades agreed, but only if Hercules was able to best Cerberus without weapons. The mighty demigod wrestled the guard dog into submission with his bare hands, defeating it with ease. He then chained the massive hellhound. Despite a colossal struggle from Cerberus, Hercules was able to drag him throughout Greece. He paraded the dog through cities and at last presented it to Eurystheus, the ruler who had challenged Hercules with the labor. In some versions of the story, Hercules then returned Cerberus to the underworld. In other versions of the tale, the hellhound escaped on his own and made his way back to his underworld home.

In two other stories, Cerberus is charmed into allowing the living to enter the underworld. Greek mythology tells of a talented poet named Orpheus, the most gifted of his age. Orpheus' wife was bitten by a poisonous snake and died. When he found her body, the musician was overwhelmed with grief. He was determined to travel to the underworld and beg for his wife to be returned to life. Orpheus played beautiful music as he traveled – music so beautiful that it beguiled Cerberus into letting him pass unharmed. His music also charmed Hades and Persephone, the ruling couple of the underworld. They agreed to let his wife Eurydice return to the land of the living, but only if Orpheus did not look back at her during the entire trip to the surface. Unfortunately, Orpheus' doubts got the better of him. Near the entrance to the above world, he glanced back at his wife to make sure she was there. Because of his lack of faith, Eurydice was condemned to stay in the underworld. Though Orpheus' journey was unsuccessful, it demonstrated that beauty could sway even the hearts of those in the realm of the dead. Despite Cerberus and Hades' fearsome reputations, a lovely song was enough to make them bend the rules.

Cerberus was also present in Roman mythology. Psyche underwent many trials to win the approval of Venus, goddess of love and mother of Psyche's beloved Eros. For one of those trials, she needed to enter the underworld. Through divine guidance, she was warned that getting past Cerberus would be impossible without a proper offering. Psyche was told to bring barley cakes sweetened with honey to tempt the dog. Upon seeing the living woman approaching him, Cerberus growled and grew agitated. However, as soon as the honey cakes were placed before him he calmed himself and devoured them. Sated by the sweet food, Cerberus ignored Psyche and allowed her to pass into the underworld unscathed.

Both the Greco-Roman Cerberus and the Norse Garmr stood as guards to the entrance of the underworld. This similarity could easily be explained away, but the fact that both were able to be lulled into submission with an offering of honey cakes seems an odd coincidence. There was little to no contact between Nordic groups and the Greeks or Romans during the times in which these stories originated. The odds of them exchanging and adapting their stories through trade seem slim to none. How, then, do two such different cultures come to possess myths with such obvious similarities?

The answer may be simple. In modern times, owners give their dogs treats to calm them down. While bones and scraps of meat were more traditional treats for dogs in early civilizations, perhaps they also devoured sweet cakes. Did both cultures evolve these stories and give the fearsome guard dogs their version of doggy treats to placate them?

Celtic mythology also featured dogs guarding the passage into another world. Instead of the underworld, their hounds stood guard over the Otherworld. This mysterious realm lay just beyond the borders of mankind's world. Some mortals were able to cross over the boundary lines, either through power, because the gods allowed it, or by stumbling across it accidentally. Time was said to move differently in the Otherworld. No one aged while there. It was a place of feasting and merriment, a look at the world as it was before mankind entered it and corrupted it. This Otherworld was called Annwn. While Annwn was a lovely place, its hounds were to be feared above all else. Called the Cŵn Annwn, or "the hounds of Annwn", their growls alone were enough to strike terror into the hearts of men. Hearing the Cŵn Annwn was usually considered to be a portent of death. Once the hounds were released on the hunt, they continued until their prey had been caught.

Beyond the regular hunting of animals or intruders in Annwn, there was a greater hunt presided over by Arawn, the ruler of Annwn. In early legends, Annwn was viewed as a lovely place, ruled over well by its just and fair king. Yet later myths, especially once the influence of Christianity reached Wales, painted a different picture entirely. Annwn was no longer an Otherworld, but an underworld closer to the Christian idea of Hell. Arawn was responsible for dragging the souls of the damned into Annwn. This task was done through an event known as the Wild Hunt.

The Wild Hunt appears in numerous mythologies, and its leaders vary depending on where the tale is told. Nordic myths set Wodan, another name for Odin, as its leader. Parts of Europe, including Germany, had their own versions of the Wild Hunt. In the early Welsh legends, the Wild Hunt involved Arawn taking a hunting party and the Cŵn Annwn on a hunt. They rode through the skies, hunting migrating geese and other prey. The Wild Hunt was also described as a way to round up lost souls, putting an end to their wandering and taking them to Annwn. Yet this myth evolved as Christianity entered the land. Later versions of the tale made the Wild Hunt a terrifying event. Those who heard the cries of the hounds must outrun the hunt or else be swallowed up by it, condemned to Annwn forever. Arawn and his Cŵn Annwn chased down the souls of the damned and overran them, dragging them back to Annwn. They were swift, fierce, and merciless.

Given the number of myths about dogs guarding the passage to the underworld, it is no surprise that European folklore latched onto the idea and created the concept of the Hellhound. Hellhounds existed in numerous cultures, including many with strong Christian influences. These dogs were described in fearful terms: massive, with black fur, sometimes bloodstained, and eyes which glowed red. They were said to lurk near graveyards or in the woods. Seeing a Hellhound was an omen of death or grave misfortune. Yet not all Hellhounds were dire creatures. Examples include the Grim, which guarded over churches and looked after their wellbeing.

It is tempting to include the Chinese mythological creatures known colloquially as Foo Dogs within this section. On the surface, these Buddhist creatures seem to fit. They were known for standing as guardians before an entrance. For hundreds of years, statues of them bedecked the boundaries of those rich enough to afford to have them carved or waited at the entrances of temples and government buildings to protect that which lay within. These dogs came in pairs, one male, and one female, and were placed on either side of a doorway. However, Foo Dogs are not, in fact, dogs. The term is a bastardization of their true nature. While they *were* guardians of boundaries, their true name was shíshī, meaning stone lion. The use of leonine creatures as protectors and guardians was a recurring theme throughout many eastern countries, with creatures similar to the shíshī appearing in Japan (where they were known as the Komainu), Korea (where they were called the Haetae), and Myanmar (which knew them as the Chinthe), among others. Leonine guardians of temples also appear in both Egyptian and Greek mythologies in the form of the Sphinx.

While the use of dogs as guardians of the underworld is extremely widespread, it is also a myth with logical reasoning behind its origin. Real life showed that dogs were the perfect creature to keep watch over an entrance. Hounds guarded homes while their masters slept. Dogs also worked alongside shepherds to herd animals where they needed to go. As such, it seems logical that a dog would sit at the entrance to another world, guarding it for its master. When necessary, the hound would herd souls into the afterlife, such as the Cŵn Annwn did during the Wild Hunt. The prevalence of this myth across cultures seems startling at first, and yet closer examination shows that dogs were chosen to guard the underworld for a logical reason.

Fate

What does fate have in store for mankind? This is a question still asked by many in the modern world. Zodiac horoscopes and astrological signs remain popular ways of determining what events lurk in the near future. Fortune cookies are a staple at restaurants around the world. Theologians and other scholars question the purpose of the universe, of mankind, and of the role humanity plays in our world. People attempt to predict what will happen during an election, which team will win in a sports match, and whether war will break out. The weather forecast, while more accurate than ever before, grows more unsure the further ahead it is predicted – and yet people want predictions. Mankind wants to know what to expect before it happens.

If such questions are still asked today, is it any surprise that fate was a much-discussed topic across many civilizations of the past? Science is turned to for many answers in the modern world, but there yet remain those who look to the stars, or to their deities, for hints of the future. In the past, most cultures believed omens and symbols to be everywhere. The gods spoke, and if one listened closely enough, they could gain some understanding of what was yet to come. Rituals and ceremonies were invoked to determine whether one should marry, or whether a country should go to war; if the harvest would be fruitful, or how many children one would have; whether an investment was wise, or if a ship would never make it to the harbor. It was believed that the gods knew all things which would occur. Moreover, deities could influence events if they were given suitable offerings.

Yet in several cultures, even the gods were not above fate. Their role in history was scripted, and there was nothing that they could do to alter that which was fated to come. A goddess who loved a mortal who perished was unable to return him to life because fate had decreed his death. A powerful god, chief among his pantheon, must live with the knowledge of how he would die until the fated day arrived. How is it that even the gods, mighty as they were, were unable to circumvent fate? What is this strange power which controlled them, and rendered even their tremendous powers impotent?

Eerily, many cultures reached the same conclusion as to the embodiment of Fate. Across numerous mythologies Fate was represented by three women, often sisters. Sometimes they represented time; in other stories, they also symbolized death. They could be weavers, or spinners, or those who cut the thread of life. These three women seemed innocuous, especially compared with the impressive elemental fury in the abilities of other gods. Yet it was they who were the most powerful, and their domain that which could not be overruled by any other living being. Even the gods feared the Fates, for early mythologies viewed Fate to be the most powerful force in the universe.

In Norse mythology, Fate was personified by the Norns. These three sisters represented that which was, that which is, and that which will be. Urdr was the eldest, and she symbolized the past. She was frequently depicted as looking over her shoulder. Verdande was the middle sister and represented the present with a straight-facing gaze. The youngest sister, Skuld, was the one who saw the future. She was shown as a mysteriously veiled woman and was frequently depicted holding a scroll. Norse mythology said that time did not exist until the Norns entered the universe and that they brought it with them. Interestingly, the Norns were not depicted as goddesses; some myths credit them as hailing from the land of the giants, while others do not explain what they were or where their powers came from.

It was the responsibility of the Norns to tend to Yggdrasil, the tree upon whose branches lie all realms. They made their home among the World Tree's roots and watered them carefully to prevent any rot from spreading. The image of the Norns was also inextricably entwined with thread. In some stories they were portrayed as weavers; Urdr spun the thread, Verdandi carded it, and Skuld wove it. In others, they were merely associated with the drawing, measuring, and cutting of thread. These threads represented the lives of all living things. When a thread was cut, the life it stood for ended. Some myths said that the Norns appeared whenever a child was born to determine their fate and to measure the length of their thread. An archaic word for fate was "wyrd", later spelled "weird", and so later portrayals of the Norns sometimes referred to them as the Weird Sisters.

Even the gods were subject to fate, and the Norns measured the strings of all the deities. Many were fated to be cut during Ragnarok. Because of the power the Norns possessed over the rest of the Norse pantheon, they were treated with enormous respect and revered by the gods. Thanks was sometimes offered to the Norns after triumph in battle; a loss could be attributed to the Norns' design. Skuld was sometimes referred to in terminology similar to a valkyrie, since it was she who determined when a man was to die, and so selected those who would die upon the battlefield.

This idea of three goddesses associated with death, battle, and fate is echoed in Celtic mythology. There Fate was represented in the form of the Morrigan. While the Morrigan is referred to using singular pronouns, she was a goddess made up of three women. They were almost always referred to as sisters, though whether they were related by blood or by marriage varied. Who those women were depended upon who told the story. The goddess Anand was almost always one face of the Morrigan, while her other two personifications could be Badb, Macha, or Nemain. Each of these goddesses individually represented war in some way but combined formed the Morrigan. On their own, they were also deities of birds, of the harvest, of horses, or of sovereigns. While depictions of the Morrigan almost always feature only one woman, the deity was always composed of three different goddesses. Later portrayals of her sometimes showed her as the Maiden, the Mother, and the Crone.

The Morrigan was revered as a goddess of war. Her favor was immensely desirable and greatly cultivated among warriors, while her wrath or displeasure was feared above all else. Those who the Morrigan sided with were fated to win in whatever battles they entered. Because of this Lugh Long-Arm, one of the mightiest heroes of Celtic mythology, made sure to win over the Morrigan's favor before attacking one of his enemies. For those who the Morrigan chose to deny her favor, the battle would be deadly. She could fog the mind of a man at war, confusing his heart and soul in the midst of the battlefield. Such unlucky souls always wound up dead.

Sighting the Morrigan before a battle was usually seen as a portent of doom. She could appear in several ways. The Morrigan was said to possess the ability to shapeshift into a bird of some sort – usually a crow. Crows, being carrion birds, were viewed as a sign of war and death. Seeing one circling above a battleground meant that many would soon die and would become a feast for the crows. If the Morrigan appeared as one of the blackbirds, it meant that battle would soon ensue...and often, those who had seen her would be dead. In an even more grim fashion, the Morrigan could also appear as a beautiful woman sitting beside a riverbank or lake. A warrior might see her washing his armor of bloodstains and would know that his next combat would be his last. More violent versions of this myth say that the Morrigan was washing the entrails of the warrior, all while maintaining direct eye contact. Her knowledge of fate was absolute. None could escape the Morrigan.

Returning to the common story element of the thread, one finds the Greek Moirai. These three goddesses were collectively known as the Fates, but their name more literally translates to "the apportioners". The parentage of the Moirai varied depending on the myth and the time. Originally, they were said to be the daughters of Nyx, goddess of night. Nyx was also the mother of Thanatos, god of death, and Nemesis, the goddess of retribution. In this aspect, fate was seen as something to be feared, or at least viewed apprehensively. Other stories attributed the Moirai as the children of Zeus, chief among the gods, and Themis, the goddess of law and cosmic order. Here the Moirai were viewed as a natural part of the universe. They maintained the order of things, keeping everything balanced as it needed to be – both among mankind and among the gods. None could escape the law of Fate. Later myths attributed the Moirai as the daughters of Ananke, the goddess of necessity or inevitability. Fate was viewed as part of the domain of their mother, something unavoidable and necessary for the good of all.

The three sisters who formed the Moirai were Clotho, Lachesis, and Atropos. Clotho was responsible for spinning the threads of every living thing. Because it was she who created an individual's thread of life, Clotho was also the one who chose the time of that person's birth. Depictions of Clotho frequently showed her holding either a spindle or a scroll, upon which was written the fates of mankind. Lachesis, the second Moirai, was the one who measured the strings and determined the length of a person's life. She was sometimes called the Apportioner, and it was she who set an individual's lot in life. More than any of the others, Lachesis was the Moirai responsible for determining an individual's destiny. It was she who set what path they would follow in life from the moment of their birth. Lachesis was often depicted as holding a staff, and some artwork showed her in connection to star signs and horoscopes. The final Moirai, Atropos, was the most feared of the three sisters. It was she who would cut the thread of life with her shears. When the thread was cut, the individual died. Atropos was sometimes called the Inexorable, for, in the end, she would cut all threads. Death was inevitable. Some myths attribute Atropos with the ability to choose the manner of everyone's death. Depictions of her usually featured her holding her dreaded shears, though some gave her a pair of scales or showed her near a sundial instead.

Much like the Norse Norns, the Moirai were said to appear shortly after the birth of a child to determine the course of their life – the babe's fate. Though they merely measured strings rather than weaving them, both the Moirai and the Norns were closely tied to thread. In addition, the Moirai shared with their Norse counterparts a power over the gods. Threads were measured for every living being, from the weakest mortal to the mightiest Titan. The power of the Moirai was absolute; no god, no matter how mighty, could hope to avoid what Fate had decreed. However, differences appear when the appearances of the Norns and the Moirai are contrasted. While some Norse artwork showed the Norns as three young maidens, most depicted Urdr as an old crone, Verdandi as a middle-aged woman, and Skuld as a young woman. For the Moirai, depictions most often showed them as three wizened old hags, wrinkled and fearful to gaze upon. Fate might have been inevitable, but its appearance was still fearful to the ancient Greeks.

The Moirai also possessed one fascinating similarity to the Morrigan. A few Greek writings, most notably those of Homer, referred to a singular goddess instead of a triple representation. This goddess was known as Moira. She was said to be the goddess of Fate. She was given the same duties as the Moirai – a spinner of thread, who measured lengths for all living things, and would eventually cut all threads. The word moira means "portion", and so the goddess portioned out the life lengths of all. Homer also attributed Moira as determining the course of events, not just the fates of individuals. Her power over the gods is shown in the *Iliad*. One mortal had the favor of Zeus, and the god wanted him to be victorious in battle. However, Zeus knew that Moira had fated him to die. Because of Fate's ultimate power, the god was helpless to do anything except watch with regret as the warrior fought and died. Is Moira similar to the Morrigan, in that she was a singular entity who represented three different goddesses? Perhaps. Yet in the *Odyssey* Moira was shown accompanied by three spinners. Are these the Moirai, and Moira simply a deity associated with them? Or was Moira always meant to be an artistic representation of the Moirai? It is hard to say, given that most of her appearances lie in Homer's works.

Many Greek deities were transferred over to the Roman pantheon, and the Fates were no exception. Known in Rome as the Parcae, they differed very little from their Greek counterparts. Clotho became Nona, Lachesis turned to Decima, and Atropos was renamed Morta. There was originally a Roman goddess of childbirth named Parca, and some scholars have theorized that she became absorbed into the Parcae. This is because Nona, meaning "the ninth", was invoked by pregnant women in the ninth month of their childbearing. Much like the Moirai, the Parcae appeared to a child shortly after its birth to determine its lot – or Fate – in life. This would have occurred ten months after conception, and Decima, who measured the thread of life, translates to "the tenth." Perhaps the most telling of all the names is that of Morta. To the Romans, Morta was even more feared than Atropos had been. She was not merely the one who cut the string and determined how one was to die: she was death personified. As with the Morrigan, Morta sometimes appeared ahead of the time of death as an omen or portent of what was to come. Seeing her meant that the end was near.

The Parcae, like the Moirai, were usually depicted as wizened old women. Their instruments were almost identical – a spindle for Nona, a staff or rod for Decima, and shears (or later, a scythe) for Morta. The Roman's adaptation of the Greek pantheon changed many aspects of the Greek deities that they adopted. Some were made weaker, others stronger; the needs of the Roman empire were considered, and their gods and beliefs altered to suit. Yet Fate's personification remained remarkably the same across both cultures. The Romans also kept the belief that not even the gods could alter or combat Fate. All living things were subject to what was allotted, and nothing could be done to change the course of Fate.

Three similar goddesses were present in parts of European mythology as well. Though their names varied depending on what country spoke of them, Slavic mythology featured three sisters who wove the destiny of mankind. In Russia they were known as the Rodzanicy; southern Slavic peoples knew them as the Suditse. These three goddesses were the daughters of the chief god, known as Rod or Sud depending on location. Sud was also the god of judgment. The Suditse were said to all three be young and beautiful. They appeared to a child shortly after it was born to determine its destiny. One of the sisters represented death. The second personified misfortune, illness, and injury. The third sister embodied good luck and happiness. This sister was stronger than the others, and usually had the most influence on the course of a person's life. The Suditse would appear one at a time before the baby, and the order in which they appeared helped to determine its destiny. Parents would sometimes leave bribes for the sisters, hoping to win their favor and have a more desirable lot set for their child. No matter what order they appeared in, each sister would take her due and make her mark upon the life of the infant. Within their life, every person would experience some joy, some sorrow, and, eventually, death.

Numerous other cultures around the world have triple goddesses representing some aspect of fate or destiny. What is the reason behind this reoccurring anthropomorphism of Fate? Most easily explained is the repetition of three deities. The modern world still has people who swear by lucky numbers. Various cultures have numbers they deem favorable, and others that they believe to be ill-fated. Seven has long been a popular number believed to bring good luck; the number thirteen is sometimes viewed with superstition in the western world, where it is believed to be bad luck. Some sects of Christianity consider 666 to be immensely unlucky, for it is said to be the number of the Beast or the Devil. Japanese culture sometimes avoids the use of the number four, since the word for it, "shi", is part of their word for death. When four must be spoken of, it is frequently called "yo" instead.

Similar concepts existed in the ancient world. Seven was a number associated with greatness. Certain cultures believed that to be the seventh son of a seventh son meant that one would have a great fate. Greek mythology had the Pleiades, for whom the star cluster is named. These seven sisters were nymphs eventually placed among the stars. The number seven was considered a number sacred to the Pharaoh during some time periods of ancient Egypt and was associated with the divine. Catholicism still speaks of the seven deadly sins.

Groups of three appear even more frequently in mythology, particularly in the Greek myths. Three was a number tied to power. In Greek mythology, Zeus, Poseidon, and Hades were three brothers who each ruled over a mighty realm. Their three sisters, Hera, Demeter, and Hestia, also had dominion over important parts of life. All other gods came after these two groups of three and were less powerful. Besides the Moirai, Greek mythology also had the Charities, a group of three goddesses who represented grace and virtue. Within the underworld, there were the three Furies or Erinyes. These goddesses sought vengeance upon the unjust and were particularly dangerous to oath breakers. Cerberus, the guardian of the underworld, had three heads.

Other religions also used three as a number associated with the divine, or with power. In Norse mythology, Odin underwent three hardships to gain knowledge of the future. In Christianity, Jesus rose from the grave after three days. Christianity also features the Trinity, in which the Father, the Son, and the Holy Spirit are three aspects of the same divine being. Some parts of the Roman Empire revered the Matres, or the Matrones – three women who represented motherhood. The number three appears again and again across cultures, associated with divine beings of immense power. This could explain why Fate was portrayed in groups of three.

Yet Fate was described as the ultimate power, one which affected even the gods. Why was fate personified across so many cultures in the form of three females? Most ancient civilizations which featured three goddesses of Fate were patriarchal. Even in those cultures where women were treated with respect, men ruled. So why would they attribute the most powerful force in the universe as being in the hands of women? The answer lies in how Fate and destiny are portrayed time and time again: As thread. Thread, spinning, and weaving were traditionally viewed as the domain of women. While some cultures differed in their gendered assignment of duties, most of those discussed above left the domestic work to females. Athena was the Greek goddess of weaving. Her Roman equivalent, Minerva, was also a deity associated with crafts and weaving. In Norse mythology, Odin's wife, Frigg, was regarded as the goddess of spinning. Another Norse deity, Holda, was the patron goddess of weavers. These goddesses also ruled over other aspects of life, ranging from harvest and fertility to warfare and tactics. Yet weaving was traditionally represented in mythology as a job for women.

Because early mythologies described Fate in terms of thread, spinning, or weaving, it makes sense that they would have women in control of Fate. It was females who traditionally handled the spinning and weaving of thread. To have a male deity untangling and spooling thread would have been greatly out of place for the time period. As such, Fate fell into the hands of women. Because of the way this most powerful of forces was thought of by early civilizations, women were depicted as being in control of the destiny of all mankind.

Flood

Throughout many cultures, there is one story which appears time and time again: the Great Flood narrative. The details in all versions bear a remarkable similarity. In it, mankind turns away from the gods and angers them with their corruption and depravity. In retaliation, a massive flood is sent to earth to exterminate all of mankind...all, that is, save for one family. This family, sometimes with children, sometimes only a husband and wife, have remained pure despite the corruption of their brethren. In recognition of their inherent goodness, a deity descends to warn them about the coming disaster. The family builds a boat or climbs aboard a log or something which floats. When the flood strikes, they survive thanks to the warning of the gods. While the rest of mankind is wiped out, this family endures and goes on to repopulate the earth.

Why is this myth so prolific across multiple mythologies? The answer may lie in a historical disaster discovered by geologists. Even if this is true, how did so many cultures create the same story independent of one another? Some crossover may have occurred between the Sumerian, Judeo-Christian, and Greek myths, but other societies would have recorded the story without influence from the Middle East. Why only has one couple survived across the many versions of the story? First, an examination of the tales is in order.

Perhaps the most well-known Great Flood narrative is that which is found in the book of Genesis. The Judeo-Christian recording of the event is taught around the world and has gained prominence thanks to the film *Noah*. During the early days of the earth, mankind turned away from God and became corrupted by their own desires. Evil lurked in the hearts of humanity. God, seeing this, decided that the creation of man had brought nothing but sorrow. He was determined to wipe all life off the face of the earth.

In the midst of the corruption there lived a man who was honest and true. His name was Noah. God looked upon Noah with favor, and so decided to warn him about the coming flood. God commanded Noah to construct a massive ark and provided him with very explicit instructions on its measurements. On this ark, he was to put two of every animal in creation, one male, and one female. He was also to take his wife, his sons, and their wives with him to escape the coming flood. Noah followed God's instructions and created the ark.

God caused the animals to approach Noah in pairs of male and female. He loaded them onto his ark, and his family as well. Noah closed the doors to the ark, and the flood descended. For forty days and for forty nights it rained. The flood covered all the earth, and everything not on the ark died. At last, God, seeing that humanity was no more, stopped the rain. For nearly half a year the ark floated in the water until God caused the water levels to drop. The ark came to rest against a mountainside, but the waters were still too high for the humans to disembark. Noah sent out a bird to investigate the land, but it flew back to him, having found no resting place. Again, he sent out a dove, and again it returned. Then, one day, Noah sent forth a dove and it came back with an olive branch in its hand. A week passed, and Noah sent the same dove out – but she did not return, having found a place to nest. God spoke to Noah and told him that it was safe to step out onto the land. Only then did Noah and his family leave the ark.

Noah's family received the blessing of God, who promised to make them fruitful so that they could multiply and fill the earth once more. God also made a covenant with Noah. He promised that never again would the earth be flooded and that the rainbow would stand as a symbol of this promise.

While the Judeo-Christian narrative of the Great Flood is perhaps the most well-known, the earliest known record of the flood is found in Akkadian tablets. The Atrahasis tablets describe a wise king of Akkadia named Atrahasis who survived a flood thanks to the help of the god Enki. During the reign of Atrahasis, the gods decided that the earth had grown too populous. Enlil sent droughts and famine to starve mankind in the hopes of reducing their numbers. This helped somewhat but was not enough to lower the population as much as he desired. He decided to send a massive flood to wipe out humanity. Knowing that he disapproved of the plan, Enlil swore Enki to secrecy. However, the clever god was able to figure out a way to warn Atrahasis without breaking his word.

Enki spoke to Atrahasis through an oracle, warning the king of the coming disaster. He was instructed to build a boat and to gather onto it his family and animals of every kind. Atrahasis obeyed the god. When the flood arrived, he was prepared and shut himself inside the ark. For seven days the flood reigned on the earth, wiping out anyone outside of the ark. On the last day, the flood ended. Atrahasis made offerings to thank the gods and appease them. Seeing that he had survived, Enlil was furious with Enki. The god denied having broken his oath, for he had not spoken directly to Atrahasis. Enlil was forced to concede the point. The king and his family survived, and the gods never flooded the earth again.

A Sumerian tablet from just a century or two later tells a similar story about Ziusudra, one of the great kings of Sumer. Though much of this tablet is lost, the basic story remains the same. In this version, it was Enki who warned Ziusudra of the coming flood. Fragments of his instructions survive, in which he told Ziusudra to fashion a boat to keep him safe. Parts of the text describe the massive deluge of the flood, which ended after seven days. Ziusdura opened a window to look at the sky. He offered a sacrifice to the gods, thanking them for his life and begging them to show mercy. The gods caused Ziusudra's boat to be grounded in a specific land, and no more of the tablet exists.

Perhaps the most famous Great Flood narrative to come out of Mesopotamia is that found in the *Epic of Gilgamesh*. This story may predate the tale of Atrahasis and could have been the inspiration for it. Small sections of tablets dating back to the 21st century BC have survived, but only parts of them can be read. Additional tablets from the 18th century BC fill in more of the story, but not all of them remain intact. The fullest stories which have been translated are found in tablets from the 13th and 7th centuries BC. The *Epic of Gilgamesh* has been found on tablets written in Sumerian, Babylonian, Akkadian, and Assyrian. Some of the cultures added their own legends onto stories already told. As such, it is difficult to say when the Great Flood narrative first appeared in the *Epic of Gilgamesh*.

Gilgamesh's story is a lengthy saga involving numerous quests, trials, and struggles with the gods. It is not he who survives the Great Flood; rather, he goes on a quest to meet the man who lived through the watery wrath of the gods. Utnapishtim was the survivor, and he had been granted everlasting life.

When Gilgamesh found Utnapishtim during the king's quest for eternal life, the old man warned him that it was not all it was cracked up to be. Gilgamesh had come to Utnapishtim to try and learn how to live forever. His best friend, Enkidu, had recently died, and Gilgamesh feared his own mortality. When he asked Utnapishtim how he had come to be immortal, the old man related his tale.

The god Ellil had decided to wipe out mankind with a flood. Ea, though sworn to secrecy, related this news to Utnapishtim through an oracle. He told him to construct a boat and gave instructions as to how it was to be built. The craftsmen of the city aided Utnapishtim in the building of the boat. He loaded it with animals of all kinds, with his family, with seed, and gold, and treasure. In addition, the craftsmen were brought on board to survive the flood. Then darkness descended upon the land. All light was snuffed out, and the storm descended. A tempest raged over the earth. It was so fierce that even the gods feared for their lives.

Seven days passed before the storm ceased. It struck the gods then what they had done when they saw their creations lying dead in the water. They wept that it had come to this. Utnapishtim too cried as he considered the death of the rest of mankind. The boat that Utnapishtim and his family had sheltered in grounded against a mountain. For seven days they remained there, waiting to see if the boat would move. On the seventh day, Utnapishtim released a dove. It flew out over the ocean but could find no place to land, and so it returned to him. The next day he released a swallow, which also found no resting place. Finally, he released a raven; it found that the waters had receded and was able to land and eat. Then Utnapishtim recognized that he was safe and made offerings to the gods.

When Ellil saw that Utnapishtim and his family had survived the flood, he was furious. He confronted Ea, suspecting that the other deity had somehow warned Utnapishtim despite his vow of silence. Ea argued that he had not broken his vow, for he had only appeared to Utnapishtim indirectly. He also chastised Ellil for the method he had chosen to wipe out mankind. Ellil realized that he had overstepped. The god approached Utnapishtim and his wife and blessed them. They were given eternal life and sent to dwell in a far-off land near the rivers. It was in that land that Gilgamesh eventually found Utnapishtim. The king's quest for immortality was ultimately futile, despite Utnapishtim relating his story to him.

For the Greeks, the story of the Great Flood revolved around Deucalion and Pyrrha. Pyrrha was the daughter of Epimetheus and Pandora and had married Deucalion, the son of Prometheus. Their story is set during the Bronze Age. In this time of mankind, humanity had grown wicked. All the greed, envy, and hate released from Pandora's box had filled the world and corrupted the hearts of men. Zeus looked upon the gods' creations with disgust. Despairing of any hope for them, he decided to wipe them all out with a massive flood.

Yet Deucalion and Pyrrha were good and devout followers of the gods. Prometheus, even while imprisoned for his crime of stealing fire, caught word of Zeus' plans. He sent a warning to his son. When Deucalion heard that a torrential flood was coming to exterminate mankind he feared for their safety. At his father's suggestion, he and Pyrrha constructed a chest and sought shelter within it. Zeus opened the heavens and the rain began to fall. Poseidon, the god of the ocean, sent waves to drown out mankind. Yet Pyrrha and Deucalion survived, for the chest they hid in floated above the water. For nine days Deucalion and Pyrrha's chest coasted above the waves. They were kept safe thanks to Prometheus' warning.

At last, the rains died away, and all life save for them was no more. The chest they had sought shelter in grounded against a mountaintop. Deucalion and Pyrrha disembarked onto the mountain. They made offerings to Zeus and the other gods, thanking them for their lives. Despite this, the mortals were filled with despair. Out of all the earth, only they were left alive. The couple wept.

Seeing their sorrow, the god Hermes descended with a message for them. They were told to throw the bones of their mother over their shoulders and to not look back. Deucalion and Pyrrha were confused until they realized that the deity meant the earth mother. Each seized a handful of rocks and threw them behind their head. Where each rock fell, a mortal sprang to life – males for the rocks Deucalion threw and females for those thrown by Pyrrha. In this way, the two mortals repopulated the earth, and humanity was restored.

The level of repetition in these stories may seem unnecessary, but it serves to demonstrate just how remarkably similar the Great Flood narratives were to one another. The birds in Utnapishtim's story mirror those found in the book of Genesis. Some theories say that the Great Flood narrative originated in Mesopotamian mythology. Through trade and oral traditions, it traveled to other nearby civilizations, including the Jews and the Greeks. Religious syncretism means that stories from one society often merge with those of another. In addition, many cultures took stories or deities they liked from other groups and made them their own. Mesopotamian mythology possessed the goddess Ishtar, a deity much like the Sumerian Inanna, and mythology experts can trace a path from those two to Aphrodite and Venus. All were the goddesses of love and were represented by the planet now called Venus. There are many other examples of ideas traveling from one culture to another, including the large cult of mystery worship for the Egyptian deity Isis in Greece and Rome.

So, did the story of the Great Flood become so prevalent due to sharing between cultures? Was the tale of one society appropriated by others and propagated throughout their religion? Another theory, one with some archaeological evidence behind it, says that a massive flood did occur near the region occupied by the Mesopotamian civilizations, the Greeks, and the Jews. There is evidence that approximately seven thousand years ago the Black Sea flooded. Geologists proposed in the early nineties that this flooding may have been caused by melting icecaps, resulting in a catastrophic rise in water levels. The Black Sea is near enough to both ancient Mesopotamia, Greece, and Israel that societies in those areas could have experienced the flooding and created stories about it.

Yet other societies also have tales similar to the Great Flood narrative, despite being a great distance from those already discussed. Hinduism tells the story of the mighty king Manu, who was immensely devout and powerful. One day while Manu was praying near a river he was approached by a small fish. It begged him to take pity on it and grant him shelter. Manu was a kind man, and so he took the fish home with him and gave it a small cup to live in. Yet the fish soon outgrew the cup, and so Manu put it in a tank. When it grew too large for that, the king transferred the fish to a river. Not too much time passed before the fish became too big even for the river, and so Manu transferred him to the ocean. Then, satisfied by the kindness and humility the king had shown him, the fish revealed his identity to Manu. The fish was, in fact, an avatar of Vishnu, one of the highest deities in the Hindu pantheon.

Vishnu's avatar warned Manu that a massive flood was coming to purge the world. Having tested Manu and found him worthy, the avatar commanded him to build an ark. On this boat, he was to put seeds of all kinds, his family, sages, and lots of rope. Manu did as he had been instructed. The ark was hastily built and loaded with all that the god had commanded. When the flood came Manu was prepared, and he, his family, and the rishi – the wise men – rested safely in the ark. Then Vishnu – or, by some accounts, Brahma, the creator god – appeared to him in the form of a massive horned fish. Manu fastened some of the ropes around the fish, which then began to pull the ark. The entire world was covered in water, with all other living things destroyed. They remained on the ark for a long time, until at last the deity towed it all the way to a distant mountaintop. There the ark was secured with rope. Manu and his family disembarked in that place and received the blessing of the god. The rishi ensured that the wisdom of the gods remained known, while Manu's family repopulated the earth.

Some other societies possess stories of a Great Flood but do not have the part where one family survived to repopulate the earth. Chinese history and mythology tell the story of Yu the Great, one of the mightiest emperors of China. For generations, the land had been plagued by massive flooding along the Yellow River. Various individuals had been tasked by rulers with controlling the flooding. Attempts were made to barricade the river, blocking off the path of the water with various dikes and dams. Though this failed, subsequent administrations continued to build the dams higher and higher, hoping that it would eventually work. Areas were evacuated, and populations were relocated, all in an attempt to keep the citizens and farmlands safe from the flooding. Nothing succeeded, and the flooding continued unfettered.

Then Yu was placed in command of the flooding. Historical records say that Yu attempted to divert the Yellow River instead of blocking it. Abandoning the dikes and dams, Yu instead had channels and drainage systems created. These lowered the levels of the river, transferring some of the waters to other rivers. Mythology tells the same story but says that Yu was aided in his construction of the water passages by various mythological creatures. Because the gods blessed him, the river ceased to flood and followed his desires. In some stories, Yu also had to fight a monster responsible for the flooding. Only when he had defeated it and taken its head as a trophy was he able to control the river.

Though many legends have been attributed to him, Yu was a historical figure in China, a powerful and wise Emperor who established a dynasty after his triumph over the Yellow River. Numerous records exist of his deeds. Though mythology has put its own unique twist on the story of the flooding, records show that the Yellow River did indeed flood over during the time of Yu the Great's reign and that his irrigation and channeling system was implemented. Archaeologists have discovered evidence of various dams and dikes, lending credence to the stories of Yu's predecessors and their own attempts at stopping the flooding. While Chinese stories tell of great floodings, like so many other mythologies, there is proof that the tales were real.

On the other hand, some mythologies have stories in which the world is destroyed by means other than a Great Flood, only to be repopulated by two survivors. Norse mythology provides one such example. One of the main themes recurrent throughout Norse mythology is Ragnarok, a highly prophesized version of the apocalypse. The arrival of Ragnarok will herald the end of the gods. Various stories and foretellings explicitly spell out exactly what will occur during Ragnarok. The sun and the moon will be devoured. The armies of the dead will escape from Hel, the Norse underworld, and rise to combat the gods. Despite a valiant attempt by the gods to defeat their foes, they will be beset on all sides. Loki will escape from his prison, and his monstrous children will aid in killing many of the gods. To make matters even worse, fire giants led by the deadly Surtr will cross the Bifrost, the rainbow bridge of the gods, and join in the battle.

Ragnarok will end with most of the gods and their allies dead. Humanity will fare no better; all the realms, including

Midgard, in which dwells mankind, will be set on fire by Surtr. All life shall burn, leaving nothing but ash and waste behind.

Yet out of this calamity, hope arises. Though Ragnarok may seem like the end of all things given how many perish, a few stragglers emerge from the ash and rebuild civilization. The sun's daughter will shine the light of a new day upon what remains of the world. The plants will make a return, once more giving green life to all things. A few gods who had previously died will emerge from the underworld and create a new pantheon. Lastly, two humans will survive Ragnarok. When the fires of Surtr come, they will hide inside the shelter of Yggdrasil, the World Tree which holds all realms. These humans are named Lif and Lifthrasir, meaning "Life" and "Eager for Life". Lif and Lifthrasir will emerge from the tree when the flames have died down. Together, the two humans will repopulate the earth, their descendants forming a new race of humanity.

"Be fruitful and multiply"; thus did God command Adam and Eve in the book of Genesis. The idea of two people being responsible for populating the entire earth with their kin is hardly a trait unique to Judeo-Christianity. Nor is it unique to humans in the stories: some mythologies begin with only two gods, and their children eventually form the rest of the pantheon. The Great Flood narrative demonstrates that even when humanity has settled the world, their numbers grown massive, they can still be wiped out. So many cultures have stories of two individuals surviving and going on to repopulate the earth. What is it which makes the idea of two mortals going on to birth civilizations such a recurring theme across such vastly different cultures?

Perhaps the answer lies in simplicity. It is easier to think of a deity creating one or two humans in the beginning than it is to imagine a massive number of mortals springing into being. Or perhaps early society viewed these myths as a way to explain birth – the first humans came from the hands of the gods, but all others were born because of the union between man and wife. Stories of disasters wiping out the entirety of mankind could have served two purposes. They would encourage reproduction, showing that humanity had once before been nearly destroyed. Because of this, it would be important to build up the numbers of one's family, ensuring that the earth would once again be settled. This could be part of why so many of the stories of the Great Flood include the gods blessing the surviving family with fertility and commanding them to repopulate the world.

Yet it seems more likely that the Great Flood narrative served in many civilizations as a cautionary tale or a demonstration of what devotion to the gods should look like. Many versions show the surviving duo to be righteous and good. The rest of the world is so wicked that the gods decide to end it all, but two still exist who are pure of heart. They are devout, willing to heed the warnings of the gods, to make offerings in gratitude, and to obey without question. Because of this, they survive. In fact, the couple does more than merely survive – they thrive. They receive the blessing of their gods and are usually placed in positions of power over the new race of humanity which they create.

The Great Flood narrative may have been based on historical events, but it was used in many religions to convince people to devote themselves to their faith. The wicked could easily be wiped out by the wrath of the gods, but the good would be spared and blessed beyond all belief. Piety, obedience, faith, devotion; these were the hallmarks most religions demanded of their followers, and so their sacred texts included stories to inspire them in the faithful. This was likely one of the reasons for the extremely similar way so many of the Great Flood narratives are phrased. Combined with archaeological evidence of heavy flooding in many regions where the stories were told, this helps to explain why so many civilizations told stories of a massive flooding.

Sun

The sun is necessary for the world. It provides warmth, light, and nutrients needed for life to flourish and survive. While modern science has discovered just how important the sun is to the existence of humanity, early mankind also recognized its importance and worshiped the sun as such. The vast majority of ancient cultures had a deity of the sun. Summer solstice celebrated the longest day of the year; winter solstice recognized the hope that the darkness was ending, and light would soon return. When all was well, the sun was viewed as benevolent, providing light and life. Yet other stories told of a different aspect of the sun. Some cultures had myths about the sun burning too hot and scorching the earth. Others told of a time when the sun would disappear, casting the world into darkness. Both were circumstances to be feared – for while the sun was usually benevolent, it would sometimes abandon or wound mankind. In some tales the sun deity was locked in an eternal struggle against the dark; if they should lose, the world would be plunged into chaos. Stories of the sun were an integral part of many early religions.

Chinese mythology said that the world originally had ten suns. These suns were the sons of a mighty god – in some versions, their father was said to be the Jade Emperor himself. The heat from one sun was more than enough to make the planet warm. However, one day the suns decided to be mischievous and all rise at the same time. The heat this generated was far too much for the world. Lakes and rivers began to dry up, their water evaporating. Plants wilted and died almost immediately. The ground cracked, and dust rose as the suns beat down upon it. Mankind sweated and hid in the shade, praying to the gods for mercy. One by one, they began to die.

Yet their prayers were heard. The gods approached the Jade Emperor, begging him to talk his sons down. Mankind was dying, and only the retreat of the suns could stop it. Though the father tried, his sons were unwilling to listen to him. They gleefully continued to shine over the world, which was in danger of being burned to a crisp.

Left with no other options, the Jade Emperor turned to another course of action. There was a mighty archer who lived among the gods named Hou Yi. Hou Yi had been blessed with immortality. The Jade Emperor tasked Hou Yi with putting a stop to the suns' deadly mischief and saving the world from their extreme heat. Hou Yi descended to earth and immediately took action. He nocked an arrow to his bow and took aim. One shot – one kill. The first sun dropped to the earth dead. Hou Yi fired again, and again, and again. One by one the suns fell from the sky. A nearby mortal, seeing that the archer had no intention of ceasing fire, hastily removed the tenth arrow from his quiver. When the ninth sun had fallen to the ground Hou Yi reached back for another arrow and found his quiver empty. Only one sun remained in the sky.

Hou Yi returned to heaven expecting to be rewarded for his heroic actions. However, the Jade Emperor was furious that Hou Yi had murdered his sons. Somehow the mighty deity had expected the immortal archer to stop the suns without killing them. Because he had slaughtered his sons, the Jade Emperor stripped Hou Yi and his wife of their immortality and banished them to earth. Yet the deed was already done, and the world saved thanks to the bow of the mighty archer. Chinese mythology states that the reason the earth only has one sun is that of Hou Yi. That single sun was enough to keep the world warmed and lit, to nourish crops and mankind – and to not kill the earth with excessive heat.

Some tribes in Africa told a story of a time when the sun had a large family which rose with him during the day. The moon was equally bright to the sun during this time, so night and day were both luminous. The sun and the moon were frequently in competition. One day the sun invited the moon to go swimming with him. He positioned the moon down the river and told him to enter the water when it was boiling, for that heat would signify that the sun had also entered the water. As soon as he was out of sight upstream, the sun and his family set burning branches near the water and caused it to boil. Thinking that the sun was bathing, the moon entered the water. The heat was extreme. When the moon emerged, it found that it had lost most of its light. The sun appeared before it and gloated that now it was the brighter of the two.

Realizing that he had been tricked, the moon decided to take vengeance upon the sun. He bided his time. Eventually, the perfect opportunity presented itself. A terrible famine plagued the land, and there was not enough food to go around. Man, and animal alike died. The moon approached the sun and suggested that they both kill off all their wives and children, as they could not possibly feed so many mouths. The sun was persuaded to this idea. The moon told the sun to wait downstream. He would take his family upstream and slit their throats. When the sun saw the red of their blood running through the water, he would know that the deed was done, and could kill his own family.

The moon and his family disappeared upstream, but he did not kill them. Instead, he commanded them to throw handfuls of red clay into the river. Streaks of red ran downstream, passing the sun and his family. Thinking that the moon had been true to his word, the sun proceeded to kill all his wives and children. Only when the moon and his family emerged unscathed did the sun realize the bloody, awful truth. He had been tricked into murdering his own family. It is because of this that the sun stood alone in the sky every day, while the moon, though paler, was surrounded by his family of stars.

Greek mythology possessed the tragic tale of Phaethon, the son of Helios. In early Greek mythology, it was Helios who was the god of the sun. Later myths passed this role on to the deity Apollo, while Selene, Helios' sister and the original goddess of the moon, was likewise relieved of her role in mythology by Artemis, the sister of Apollo. As such, some later retellings of this myth name Phoebus Apollo as the father of Phaethon. Yet the original story belongs to Helios and Phaethon and is told as such.

Phaethon was born the son of the sea-nymph Clymene and never knew his father. His mother always claimed that his father had been one of the gods. However, she refused to tell Phaethon which one. As the boy grew up he was teased and harassed by other boys his age for his lack of knowledge concerning his father. His playmates insisted that he was not really descended from a god and that his mother had been lying to him all his life. When Phaethon returned home he confronted his mother. He demanded to know the name of his father. Clymene revealed that he was the son of Helios and told him to go and seek out his father for proof.

The boy journeyed to the palace of the sun god and was met by Helios. The god confirmed that he was Phaethon's father, and welcomed his son home. Phaethon asked for Helios to grant him one request to prove that he truly was the boy's father. The god of the sun swore upon the river Styx to do whatever the boy asked. To swear upon the river Styx was to make an oath so powerful that not even the gods could break their word. This would be the undoing of Phaethon. The boy asked to be allowed to drive his father's chariot, which moved the sun across the sky. Phaethon believed that doing so would show his playmates that he really was descended from the god of the sun. Helios desperately attempted to talk his son out of the idea. He told Phaethon that the boy would never be able to survive his daily route. The chariot was burning hot to the touch, and the horses who pulled it breathed fire. The course Helios took through the stars was full of danger, for many of the constellations were living things which would attack at a moment's notice. Despite his father's warnings, Phaethon was undeterred – and the god, having sworn upon the river Styx, could not go back on his word.

Unable to deny his son, Helios loaded Phaethon into his chariot. He warned the boy again of all the dangers. Helios also provided Phaethon with a detailed account of his route. If the boy deviated off course, the sun would be too far or too close to the earth. Too far and the world would be overcome by freezing temperatures; too near, and fire and heat would reign. Either would be disastrous. Having done the best he could, and left with no other recourse, Helios handed Phaethon the reins. The horses took off, flying through the dark sky. Their light heralded the rising of the sun on earth. For a few moments all was well; then calamity struck. The horses did not feel the usual tight grip of their master on the reins. They reared and bucked, fighting Phaethon's tentative control. The boy panicked and lost his grip on the reins.

Without control, the horses deviated from the path they had taken for countless years. They veered too far from the earth. The light grew dimmer, and the earth grew cold. Without the sun's warmth, the waters began to freeze. Harvests froze and were buried in snow, and mankind suffered. Phaethon strove to regain control, but the horses had a mind of their own. They swerved closer to the earth, and closer still – too close. The heat of the sun began to consume the planet. Plants shriveled and died; deserts formed where once there had been green landscape. Lakes and rivers began to evaporate. People began to burn. Mankind turned to the gods for help, begging them to end the reign of fire. Eventually, the earth herself began to weep, begging Zeus to free her from her fiery torment.

Though he regretted the necessity, Zeus had no other choice. He flung a bolt of lightning at the chariot. The god's aim was unerring. His lighting flew true, striking the chariot and sending it crashing from the sky. Phaethon fell with it. Still aflame, they crashed into a river. Helios had kept his promise to his son, but the boy's request had cost him his life. Helios was heartbroken by the death of his son. For a time, the world remained in darkness while the god mourned. At last Zeus and the other gods were able to convince him to return to his duties, once more bathing the world in light.

The idea of a sun deity disappearing and refusing to light the world can also be found in Japanese mythology. Three deities were born of Izanagi when he cleansed himself after visiting his wife in the underworld: Tsukiyomi, god of the moon, Amaterasu, goddess of the sun, and Susanoo, god of the seas. Tsukiyomi and Amaterasu were content with their lot, but Susanoo grew jealous of his sister's power. He felt that the sun was more powerful than the sea. The god began to covet her position. After angering his father, Susanoo was banished from heaven. Before he left he attempted to trick Amaterasu, inviting her to a private meeting. The goddess was suspicious of her brother, and so went armed with a bow and quiver of arrows. At their meeting, Susanoo proposed a contest to see who truly was stronger. Though Susanoo seemed close to claiming victory, it was Amaterasu who emerged as the victor.

Enraged by this, Susanoo descended to the earth. There he began a reign of terror designed to insult his sister. He desecrated a temple dedicated to the harvest of rice, a grain which was sacred to Amaterasu. The god of the sea also summoned massive tsunamis and floods to destroy the rice paddies. His final and most vicious insults were yet to come. According to some myths, Susanoo killed one of Amaterasu's handmaidens. Most tales agree that he skinned a horse and threw the body into the chamber where Amaterasu and her handmaidens were weaving.

The goddess was horrified by the sight and fled. She sought shelter in a dark cave, hiding from the rest of the world.

Unfortunately for the world, Amaterasu was the embodiment of the sun. Without her presence, the earth fell into darkness. All grew chill without the warmth of the sun. The gods tried to convince Amaterasu to emerge, but she refused. Her fear of her brother remained too strong. Yet the longer the sun remained hidden away, the more the world suffered. Eventually, the gods came up with a plan. They placed a mirror outside of the cave and gathered around it. Then Uzume, the goddess of dancing, was summoned forth. She began to dance outside of the cave where Amaterasu was hiding. All the other gods milled about her, smiling and laughing with delight.

Amaterasu heard all of this and grew curious. She peeked out of the cave to see what was happening. The first thing she saw was her own reflection in the mirror. The gods told her that they were celebrating the appointment of a new goddess of the sun. Amaterasu did not recognize her reflection and wanted to know who this mysterious goddess was. She emerged from the cave and approached the mirror to see. As soon as she was out of the cave the gods sealed it shut with a massive boulder. Amaterasu had been tricked – and now she was unable to hide any longer. The goddess resumed her usual duties, and the sun once more lit the sky. To ensure her safety, the gods made sure that Susanoo was cast down to earth, his banishment enforced.

A more violent and bloody version of a sun deity could be found in the Aztec pantheon. Aztec civilization worshiped Tonatiuh as the god of the sun. Tonatiuh was a warrior deity, but he also nurtured humanity by providing necessary light and warmth. However, to continue aiding mankind, Tonatiuh demanded human sacrifice. Some versions of the myths say that these offerings were necessary because without them Tonatiuh would refuse to move through the sky. Not wishing to be trapped in an eternal day, the Aztecs gave the hearts of their enemies to the sun god. Other myths claim that Tonatiuh was too exhausted from being reborn each day to move and that only the hearts of warriors would give him the strength to make his daily trek across the sky.

However, most of the myths cite a battle with the forces of darkness as the reason behind Tonatiuh's eternal need for sacrifice. Each night when the sun went down Tonatiuh did combat with the night, struggling to persevere and return to light the world the next morning. The Aztecs did their best to aid their god by offering him hundreds of thousands of human sacrifices throughout the years. Worthy warriors were captured from enemy factions during the Flower Wars, and their hearts removed in a ritual. The still beating hearts were then offered to Tonatiuh. Through the strength of these mighty fighters, the god gained strength – enough to continue to persevere in his nightly battle.

A similar struggle between the light and the darkness can be found in Egyptian mythology. The god of the sun in Egypt was Ra. This god was chief among the Egyptian deities. He was the god of the earth and the sky, and the creator of all living things. Every day Ra traveled through the air on a great solar barge. This provided sunlight for all of mankind. Yet when the sun set, Ra's journey changed and became immensely dangerous. Every night Ra traveled through the underworld on another barge. His journey was fraught with danger, for within the underworld lurked a monstrous serpent. This creature was known as either Apep or Apophis.

Apophis was born out of chaos and represented all the darkest aspects of the universe. Apophis attacked Ra every night when his barge entered the darkness. Sunset heralded the beginning of an epic battle between the two cosmic beings. At times Ra was said to have the assistance of various other deities aboard his barge; other myths say that it was the sun god alone who stood against the darkness. Apophis would attack from the darkness without warning or send massive waves to try and capsize Ra's boat. It coiled about him and attempted to crush him or struck with open jaws to devour. Should the serpentine creature ever succeed in defeating Ra, the world would know eternal darkness. Yet time and time again Ra emerged triumphant from the dark night. With each morning came the rebirth of the sun, the dawn signifying Ra's victory over Apophis. Though locked in an eternal struggle, Ra was never defeated.

A cosmic battle in which the sun resists darkness was also present in Norse mythology, though it was fated to have a most bitter ending. When the world was first created the gods placed the sun and the moon in the sky. Sol was the goddess of the sun, and Mani the god of the moon. These deities rode their chariots around the world to provide light and warmth. Yet from the beginning Sol and Mani faced opposition. Two giant wolves, Skoll and Hati, chased them across the night sky. The two gods could never stop their chariots for fear of being caught by their pursuers. Throughout every month Hati drew closer to Mani, taking bites out of the moon and shrinking it. The moon regenerated, and Mani was able to stay just far enough ahead to survive.

This chase was eternal, allowing no rest for the gods. Their struggle against the wolves was fated to end in disaster. On the day of Ragnarok, it is prophesized that Hati and Skoll will, at last, overtake Sol and Mani. The sun and the moon will be devoured by the wolves. This shall cast the earth into darkness. Even the stars will fall from the sky. The battle between the forces of the gods and their enemies shall occur, and the world will end in fire. Yet out of this calamity, a new light will dawn. Somehow, despite her constant desperate efforts to escape, Sol will conceive and give birth to a daughter before her death. This new sun shall light the earth, and the survivors of Ragnarok shall gather together to create a new society. Even in the darkest of times, the ancient Norse believed that the light would prevail.

For early societies, the sun was the most important factor in their lives. It provided light to work by, warmth to live in, and made the harvests possible. The loss of the sun would have been catastrophic for early civilizations. As such, many of their myths feature stories in which the sun disappeared for a time or tell tales of mighty battles between light and darkness. In a time when only the sun or fire provided light and warmth, the loss of either was something to be dreaded. The celebration of the triumph of day over night existed even separate from the gods: The winter solstice heralded the end of the long dark days and the return of warmth and sun. The appearance of these stories across so many cultures, and the considerable similarities between them demonstrate just how integral the sun was to early peoples. It also shows how much the darkness was feared. This darkness was often given a form and a name, as in the cases of Apophis or Hati and Skoll. Because the sun was so often anthropomorphized as a deity, it possessed massive power. It would take an equally strong force to defeat it.

Fear of the dark has been a phobia throughout human history. For early cultures without access to other forms of light, and who lived near nighttime predators, it would have been particularly intense. Yet day after day the sun rose again. This common fear of the dark – and hope in the light – is the reason for the existence of so many similar myths about the sun.

Conclusion

Every culture in the world possesses stories, and early peoples were no exception. Their stories talked about what was important to them. They showed what they believed to be true, how they expected people to act, and what they hoped for or feared. By examining the myths of ancient civilizations, it is possible to determine what they believed. It can also show what roles could be found within their culture. To examine the mythology of a society is to examine every aspect of their culture.

When stories from different civilizations are compared, it becomes apparent that great similarities existed between them. Even in cases where the societies never met or did trade, they possessed similar stories. These parallels found throughout mythology show that the mind of mankind works in alike ways despite differences in cultures and values. Fire, family, and sun were cherished and viewed with gratitude. Natural disasters were looked upon with dread, and it was believed that they could be avoided if the gods were treated with due reverence. Fate was a tangled mess of strings, but there was no escape from it – for it was more powerful than even the gods. Time and again, across a multitude of cultures, stories appear reinforcing these and other themes.

While examining the stories of an individual society can produce great insight into that particular culture, an examination of stories across all civilizations provides insight into man itself. It shows that geography affects the stories that a group tells, and the deities they believe in. It proves that gendered roles are depicted in mythology through the gods and the heroes portrayed within and the roles that they play. Faith and trust in the gods are shown time and again across mythology. The very stories of their religions urged early people to believe and to have faith and promised that the gods would reward those who did. Mythology also promised punishment for those who turned away from the gods, or who chose a life of depravity. A closer look at mythology shows that not all myths are pure fiction, as historical characters from numerous cultures have been worked into their mythologies – from Gilgamesh in Mesopotamia and Emperor Yu in China to Roman emperors such as Romulus. Colossal events such as natural disasters are also worked into mythology. Perhaps they are exaggerated to make them seem even direr, but their stories are still a reflection of the truth.

Mythology also acted as a reflection of real and everyday life. Just as fire can be both a blessing or a danger in the hands of man, it was portrayed as either benevolent or violent in myths depending on how it was used. Mankind tasks dogs to act as guardians of the home or help herd animals and aid shepherds; in mythology, the gods set hounds to stand as guards at important boundaries and shepherd the souls of the dead. Ideal roles and actions are demonstrated by the gods and heroes, giving a model for those who believe in them to follow. Characters whose actions

One Last Thing

If you enjoyed this book, you can help me tremendously by leaving a review on Amazon. You have no idea how much this would help.

I also want to give you a chance to win a **$200.00 Amazon Gift card** as a thank-you for reading this book.

All I ask is that you give me some feedback. You can also copy/paste your *Amazon* or *Goodreads review* and this will also count.

Your opinion is super valuable to me. It will only take a minute of your time to let me know what you like and what you didn't like about this book. The hardest part is deciding how to spend the two hundred dollars! Just follow this link.

http://booksfor.review/samestories

[page intentionally left blank]